11/17

Earthworms

Leo Statts

abdopublishing.com

Published by Abdo Zoom™, PO Box 398166, Minneapolis, Minnesota 55439. Copyright © 2018 by
Abdo Consulting Group, Inc. International copyrights reserved in all countries. No part of this book may be
reproduced in any form without written permission from the publisher. Abdo Zoom™ is a trademark and logo
of Abdo Consulting Group, Inc.

Printed in the United States of America, North Mankato, Minnesota
052017
092017

Cover Photo: iStockphoto
Interior Photos: iStockphoto, 1, 4–5, 9, 10–11, 15, 18; Shutterstock Images, 6, 7; Constantin Cornel/iStockphoto,
8; Red Line Editorial, 11, 20 (left), 20 (right), 21 (left), 21 (right); Jacana/Science Source, 13; J. L. McLoughlin/
iStockphoto, 14; blickwinkel/Hecker/Alamy, 17; M. B. Cheatham/iStockphoto, 19

Editor: Brienna Rossiter
Series Designer: Madeline Berger
Art Direction: Dorothy Toth

Publishers Cataloging-in-Publication Data
Names: Statts, Leo, author.
Title: Earthworms / by Leo Statts.
Description: Minneapolis, MN : Abdo Zoom, 2018. | Series: Backyard animals |
    Includes bibliographical references and index.
Identifiers: LCCN 2017931122 | ISBN 9781532120046 (lib. bdg.) |
    ISBN 9781614797159 (ebook) | ISBN 9781614797715 (Read-to-me ebook)
Subjects: LCSH: Earthworms--Juvenile literature. | Invertebrates--Juvenile
    literature.
Classification: DDC 592--dc23
LC record available at http://lccn.loc.gov/2017931122

Table of Contents

Earthworms

Earthworms are invertebrates.

They are soft and slimy. They spread air and **nutrients** through soil.

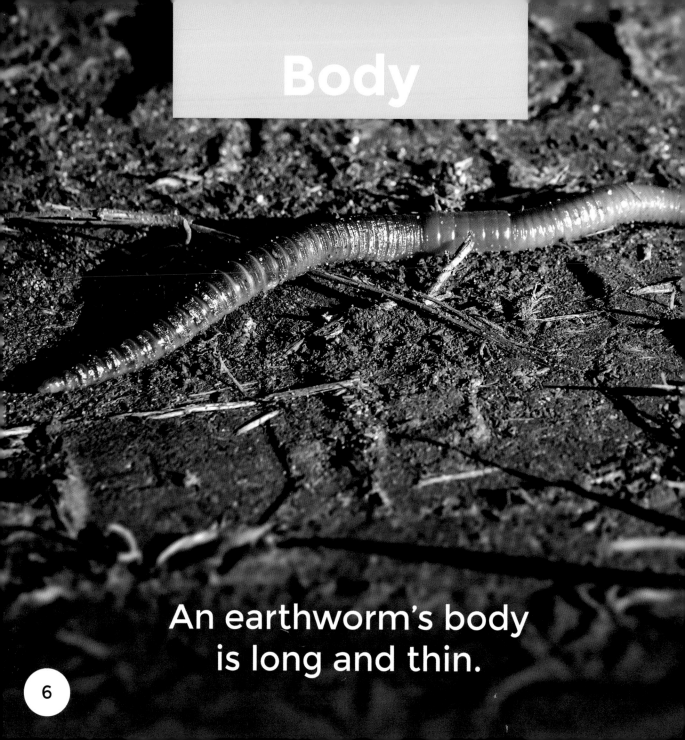

Body

An earthworm's body
is long and thin.

It has sections
that look like rings.

Each section has many stiff hairs.

The hairs help the earthworm move.

Habitat

Earthworms live all over the world. They dig tunnels through the dirt.

Where earthworms live

Most tunnels are not very deep. But some go more than six feet (1.8 m) underground.

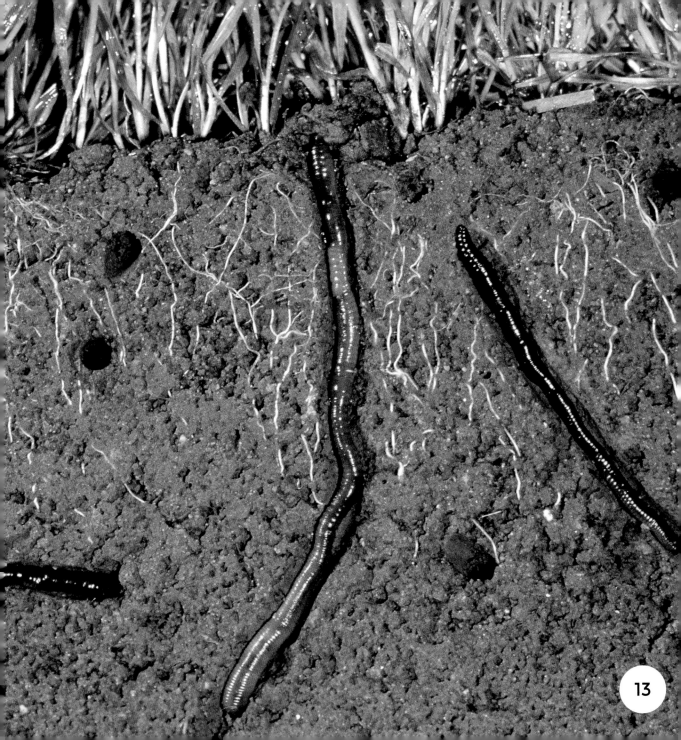

Food

Earthworms eat dirt as they dig. Plant parts are in the dirt. Earthworms digest the plants.

Then the dirt leaves their bodies as droppings.

Life Cycle

Adult earthworms make **cocoons**. Each cocoon has eggs in it.

Tiny earthworms **hatch** from the eggs. They look like small adults.

Earthworms live for
six to eight years.

Average Length – Shortest

The smallest earthworm is slightly longer than a penny.

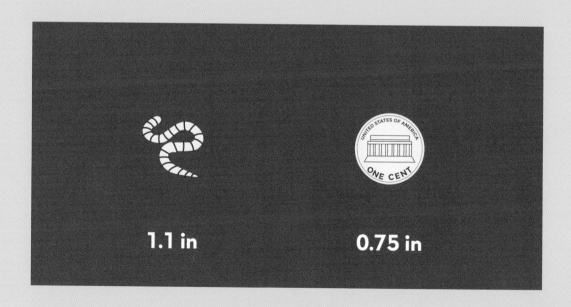

1.1 in   0.75 in

Average Length – Longest

A giant Gippsland earthworm is shorter than an acoustic guitar.

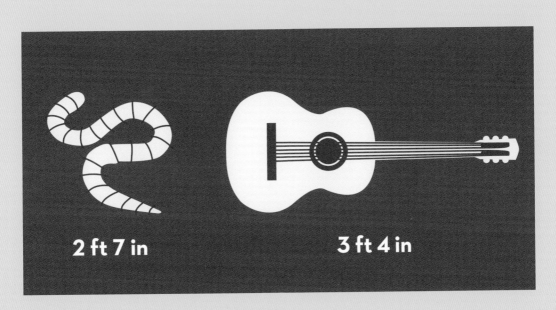

2 ft 7 in   3 ft 4 in

Glossary

cocoon - a covering that protects an animal's eggs or a growing animal.

digest - the process of breaking down food.

hatch - to be born from an egg.

invertebrate - an animal without a backbone.

nutrient - something that helps plants or animals live and grow.

Booklinks

For more information on **earthworms**, please visit abdobooklinks.com

Zoom™ In on Animals!

Learn even more with the Abdo Zoom Animals database. Check out **abdozoom.com** for more information.

Index